DISCIPLINE AND DIRECTION

DISCIPLINE AND DIRECTION

GOD'S LEADERSHIP STYLE

TERRY STEPHENS

J MERRILL

All scripture quotations not otherwise identified are from the King James Version of the bible.

J Merrill Publishing, Inc.
434 Hillpine Drive
Columbus, OH 43207
www.JMerrill.pub

Library of Congress Control Number: 2023906416
ISBN-13: 978-1-954414-91-4 (Paperback)
ISBN-13: 978-1-954414-92-1 (eBook)
Book Title: Discipline and Direction: God's Leadership Style
Author: Terry Stephens
Cover Artwork: Safeer Ahmed

CONTENTS

INTRODUCTION

Many leaders, pastors, parents, teachers, youth leaders, grandparents, aunts, uncles—and especially single mothers—are facing significant challenges with the current generation of children and young adults. So significant are these problems that businesses are restructuring themselves or shutting down because of a dearth of competent employees. We see children having children. This is a generation characterized by rebelliousness, argumentativeness, and irresponsibility. I am not a medical doctor, but based on my interactions with this generation, I attribute these behaviors largely to a lack of discipline. Here, I refer to discipline in terms of physical actions, mental thoughts, and feelings—all of which require discipline. I believe this lack stems from what can best be described as fatherlessness.

There's a reason we call a father "dad" in our society: the acronym stands for Discipline and Direction. Many of this generation's issues can be mitigated by reintroducing "Dad" (Discipline and Direction) into their lives. This book serves as a five-step guide to transform this generation of rebellious, argumentative, and irresponsible young adults and children into highly motivated, productive citizens who embody confidence, discipline, and direction. That's right: bringing Discipline and Direction ("Dad") back is crucial.

According to the U.S. Census Bureau, twenty-four million children in America—one out of three—live in homes without their biological fathers. The insights you will find in this book aim to educate you on relating to this generation and eliciting the best from them. These young adults and children are not compliant robots; your adolescent teenager is not your drinking and smoking buddy.

This generation is akin to fish in a lake being forced into the ocean: the transition, while exciting, is also confusing. Life and the economy are ever-changing, undergoing transitions even as we speak. This generation cannot step into adulthood and the workforce unaided; they must be guided. Their challenges may not be more difficult than those faced by previous generations, but they are certainly more demanding. The availability of sex, drugs, and violence distinguishes this generation from its predecessors, who paved the way through inventions, talent, and education. This generation possesses just as much creativity, inventiveness, education, talent, and giftedness to propel us further. Our focus should be on attending to this fatherless generation. As you read this book, you will gain insight into how you can assist these young people in their transition to adulthood and the workforce by infusing Discipline and Direction into their lives.

DISCIPLINE AND DIRECTION

We live in a world where "discipline" has become a bad word. Of course, everyone wants to be free to do whatever they want, whenever they want, and however they want. But to live in a society like that is to invite chaos. Therefore, every society must have discipline and order—not to prevent people from doing what they want, but to protect them from harming one another or themselves. Webster's Dictionary defines "discipline" as training that corrects, molds, or perfects the mental faculties or moral character. It is also defined as control gained by enforcing obedience or order or a rule or system governing conduct or activity.

In a world where sex, drugs, and violence have reached an all-time high, discipline is in high demand. But have you ever heard the saying, "You can't teach an old dog new tricks"? Discipline is something that must be instilled at an early age. In our formative years, we learn the most, and life-altering decisions are made—even at young ages. Discipline plays a vital role for children, helping them develop self-control, respect for authority, and the ability to interact and cooperate with their peers. Discipline also makes children feel safe and loved and often determines the kind of person they will become.

Many people view discipline as synonymous with punishment or correction. However, punishment and correction are responses to bad behavior, whereas discipline prevents bad behavior. Discipline sets boundaries to protect us, not to restrict our enjoyment. Children understand this concept when they play games. All games have rules; if children can abide by those rules, they should have no problem abiding by yours. Consider how much fun children have playing sports like basketball, football, and baseball. Even video games on the PlayStation, Xbox, and computers have rules. Discipline and rules are integral parts of life, and this generation of young people is familiar with them. Our job as parents is to help them apply the same discipline they exercise in games to life.

I like to use the lines on the street as an example of discipline. These lines are not intended to restrict us but to protect us from harming ourselves and others during our journey. Can you imagine the chaos if we didn't have streetlights and lines on our roads? It would be utter chaos, making driving a traumatic experience. Just as we need streetlights and lines, we must also live disciplined lives.

I'm convinced that some people possess personal discipline, while others require systemic discipline governed by external authorities. Some people exhibit a more significant measure of self-control than others. This doesn't make them better individuals; it simply means they have matured more in the area of self-control. I've often observed that young and older people in structured environments perform better than in non-structured settings. When people have the security they need, they tend not to act out of control. This security isn't only physical necessities like food, clothing, shelter, and emotional support in the form of love, patience, and understanding.

According to Wikipedia, discipline is a life necessity. The free encyclopedia defines it as systematic instruction intended to train a person, sometimes literally referred to as a disciple, in a craft, trade, or other activity or to follow a particular code of conduct or "order." Indeed, to discipline someone means to make a disciple out of them, encouraging them to live in a manner akin to your own. This is a profound responsibility; if you don't embody the lifestyle you desire your child to lead, how can you effectively instruct them?

The "Good Book" offers an excellent example of the "DAD" (Discipline and Direction) principle. Exodus 13 states that God led the children of Israel by a pillar of cloud during the day and by a pillar of fire at night. The Bible informs us that He directed them away from the land of the Philistines to prevent them from retreating to Egypt because of the threat of war, despite this route being quicker. A loving father always considers his children's best interests. Sometimes, the fastest and easiest route isn't necessarily the best one. God used the pillar of cloud by day and the pillar of fire by night to lead the Israelites out of Egypt, through the wilderness, and into the Promised Land. This act embodies direction. This is how we—primarily fathers, parents, teachers, youth leaders, grandparents, aunts, uncles, pastors, business leaders, and so forth—should guide our young people. Our youth desperately need leadership, direction, and guidance. They aspire to succeed; they yearn to make us proud. Yet, without proper guidance, the road to success can be fraught with danger and fear, leading to considerable frustration among young people. The absence of fathers to guide them further exacerbates the situation.

The frustration of wanting to accomplish something or reach a destination without clear instructions is profound. Our appliances come with assembly instructions, as do most of our purchases. Yet life does not come with a manual, except perhaps the Bible. Even with the Bible, we require someone experienced to guide us—someone who can anticipate dangers before we become entangled in them. We need fathers who will accompany us throughout life, offering assistance along the way. In biblical times, if a man were a farmer, his son would likely become a farmer. If a man were a warrior, his son would follow suit. We no longer observe such well-defined roles. The presence of a father in a child's life, showing him the ropes, eliminates uncertainty about the child's future profession.

I deem this crucial because a child's inherent talents, often inherited from their parents, can facilitate achieving their goals. Observing their parents use these gifts offers the child a glimpse of what they could become as adults. Again, the two significant responsibilities God assigned were Discipline and Direction. God entrusted Moses with many tasks, but these two were his primary duties. If fathers took on this "DAD" role seriously, our world would undoubtedly be better.

So, how did God administer discipline? In Exodus 20, He invited Moses up the mountain to bestow upon him the Law, often condensed to the Ten Commandments. However, this Law extended beyond these commandments; it was more nuanced. It comprised three components: moral, ceremonial, and civil law.

Moral law blended justice and mercy. All stipulations of God's moral law revolve around two principles. The first is, "Thou shalt love the Lord thy God with all thine heart, and with all thy soul, and with all thy might" (Deuteronomy 6:5, King James Version). The second is, *"Thou shalt love thy neighbor as thyself"* (Leviticus 19:18, King James Version). Moral law signifies righteousness—a universal guide to ethical living. However, it cannot redeem those who breach it.

The ceremonial law governed the tabernacle, sacrificial offerings, and the priestly ministry. Each ordinance of the ceremonial law pointed toward Christ and His mission to save humanity from sin. Every function the priests performed symbolized Christ's ministry in the heavenly sanctuary. While the moral law delineated the conduct of the righteous, the ceremonial law focused on the plan of salvation and God's work of grace for the repentant, believing sinner. Through the ceremonial law, the righteousness of God could be "witnessed by the Law and the Prophets."

God provided Israel with civil regulations and the authority to enforce law and order like any country, kingdom, or state. These laws were not tribal; they were national. The people of Israel had to abide by these laws, just as we follow the laws of our respective lands.

Discipline is not about limiting our enjoyment of life. On the contrary, discipline (in the form of rules and laws) protects us from our own and others' harmful actions—much like the rules in children's games. These rules don't inhibit fun; they create an environment for it. If children can comply with the rules of their games, they can—and should—abide by your rules. Therefore, let's reintroduce Discipline and Direction into our children's lives.

My preferred method for explaining and teaching discipline is to use the lines on our streets and roads as examples. These lines don't enforce obedience; instead, they represent healthy boundaries within which we should operate—not just to reach our destination but to do so safely. This approach mirrors how discipline should be administered. God didn't prevent us from sinning; He simply established the Law to deter us from harming ourselves and others. God does not prevent sin. Sin is the transgression of the Law. If God had prevented sin, Satan could not have rebelled against Him; Adam and Eve could not have eaten the forbidden fruit, and you could not have committed your sins. God does not prevent sin. Discipline represents the boundaries we establish to help people navigate life safely. If God prevented sin, conscience would not be needed—a faculty that differentiates good from evil. We intrinsically understand right from wrong. No one teaches children to lie when they secretly take a cookie from the jar. Their conscience informs them that they are doing something wrong, yet it does not compel them to obey. You may wonder why bad things happen to people. Often, it's a consequence of their actions because GOD DOES NOT PREVENT SIN.

1

GAINING RESPECT

riends, respect is earned, not given—regardless of age, race, creed, religion, or context, be it on the job, at church, at home, or at the grocery store. I firmly believe that respect must be earned in all interactions, including those with parents, friends, bosses, coworkers, and others. Parents like yourselves must earn the respect of their children, teenagers, or young adults. Achieving this involves two methods that have proven effective in my experiences: leading troubled children and young soldiers in the Army and serving as a pastor in the church.

The first method I call the "reward-consequence" method. This technique leverages reward or consequence to motivate individuals toward desired behavior, with each instance of consequence followed by genuine parental affection (GPA)—or comfort. For example, suppose a father tells his son, "If you mow the lawn weekly, you can use my car for an hour each week. However, if you do not, you will lose the privilege of using the car." If the boy responds positively, the father must honor his word and grant the promised reward. Conversely, if the boy does not respond positively, and a consequence is necessary, it is crucial to enforce the consequence, followed by

GPA. Here, GPA serves as comfort, providing reassurance about future opportunities.

It is essential to remember that when imposing consequences, they should stem from a place of love, not anger. Moreover, showing affection the following day is crucial. Otherwise, the child might perceive the continued punishment as a sign of unforgiveness. As stated in Lamentations 3:22–23, *"The faithful love of the Lord never ends! His mercies never cease. Great is his faithfulness; his mercies begin afresh each morning."* As leaders, we should embody the principle of forgiveness, much like Jesus did for us. I am not implying that a consequence cannot last more than one day; instead, I am stressing the importance of exhibiting daily mercy, as we experience God's mercy daily.

According to Matthew 6, the penalty for unforgiveness persists until we forgive. We should administer consequences similarly. For instance, if you ask your child to clean their room on Monday and find it unclean on Tuesday, an appropriate punishment might be grounding. This grounding should last until the room is cleaned and extended to account for the task's delay. The world imposes late fees for delayed returns, so besides teaching punctuality, this strategy teaches the consequences of tardiness. Although it's important to teach our children the Bible, we live in this world and should teach them how to function within its systems. Jesus knew not only God's word but also the laws and traditions of the land, often reminding the Pharisees and Sadducees of their own laws.

Handling females may require less intensity than males, but GPA may be more critical. I am not suggesting being more lenient with females than males; since females are generally more emotionally driven, your interaction with them should cater more to their emotional needs.

Dr. Gary Chapman's book, "The Five Love Languages of Teenagers," elaborates on this concept. He explains five emotional love languages —five ways people speak and understand emotional love.

Considering females are generally more emotional than males, emphasis should be placed on GPA.

While I can speak only from a male perspective, it is crucial to proceed with caution when administering GPA to children who are not your own. Some children become emotionally attached, which could cross boundaries. The perception of such situations can sometimes harm your reputation.

Many young individuals—like my younger self—need more than words to understand and comply with instructions. I would intentionally disobey to test whether my father would uphold his words. If he had failed to do so, he would have lost credibility.

As a choleric personality type, I am task-oriented and active. Cholerics are demanding, directing, dominating, and decisive. Their primary motivation is a challenge; without it, they can become depressed or anxious. Cholerics thrive when in charge and will strive to maintain control. However, this need for autonomy is not always detrimental; cholerics excel at decision-making in high-pressure situations. To manage a choleric child, one must maintain authority at all costs. Eventually, the choleric child will grow to respect you for being assertive and decisive.

Leadership is about making decisions. One should not shy away from making decisions that might offend those under your care as long as it serves the greater good.

Okay, what if my child isn't choleric but a class clown, entertainer, or a sanguine? A sanguine personality refers to high-energy individuals who are inspiring, influential, and interested in people. They're always the life of the party or a people pleaser. Like cholerics, sanguines are motivated by recognition. They crave the spotlight and know how to attract attention. This need for recognition isn't necessarily negative; sanguines are excellent communicators and typically a joy to be around. So, how do you manage a child who is a people pleaser and loves the spotlight? First, you must learn to speak their language: charisma. A sanguine will charm you into doing what they want. Learn from them and respond in kind.

Take a lesson from the serpent. The serpent adapts to its environment to achieve its goals. For example, when a serpent moves from green to brown grass, it changes skin color to blend in. My brown skin color makes me no more or less human than a Caucasian man. This principle applies to all personalities and all people. To delve deeper, suppose we're interacting with a group of hip-hop enthusiasts. Who would command their attention and respect first: a man in a three-piece suit discussing stocks and bonds or a man in casual attire talking about investing in Jay-Z's corporation, earning a discount on his products as a shareholder, and accruing four percent interest over time? They would probably listen to the man who appears more relatable and mentions someone they're familiar with. This principle works in reverse as well. I can't approach a group of doctors using computer jargon; I need to use medical and health analogies for them to understand fully. Every person we encounter has a cultural, occupational, or hobby-based language that can assist us in communicating with them. The key is doing your research and studying those under your care.

Some young people respond to verbal discipline and won't give you problems for a while, whereas others respond only to action. If you say you'll do something, exert every effort to follow through. Trust is established by keeping your word, which is crucial for earning the respect of young people. If your youth are anything like I was, you must prove yourself consistently. Patience and consistency are two fundamental characteristics required for this method to work. Today's youth are not pushovers; they can play the game but will test you repeatedly.

Maintain consistency regarding consequences and possess enough patience to endure the testing. I once dealt with a situation involving a teenager while working at the Clark County Juvenile Detention Center in Springfield, Ohio, as a community service supervisor. One day, I had a work crew of eight teenagers working at a local middle school during the summer. One young man, particularly strong-willed, chose not to complete the task I had assigned him. I informed him that if he didn't meet the task, he would have to do so after everyone else had been dismissed. He chose not to do it, so I arranged for him to be removed from the crew until day's end. He sat in the court's lobby until I returned. I had previously coordinated with the school custodian that I would return with the young man. That day, I worked overtime for free, and the young man gave me no further problems. Sometimes, inconveniencing yourself is necessary to establish respect, but the result is worth it.

Jesus also utilized this method. In Matthew 6:14–15 (KJV), He says, *"For if ye forgive men their trespasses, your heavenly Father will also forgive you: But if ye forgive not men their trespasses, neither will your Father forgive your trespasses."* Matthew 7:1–2 (KJV) adds, *"Judge not, that ye be not judged. For with what judgment ye judge, ye shall be judged: and with what measure ye mete, it shall be measured to you again."* Notice that each action has a reward or consequence. God has attached a promise to every request He makes. He didn't lead with emotions or biases, and no favorites existed. Romans 2:11 (KJV) says, *"For there is no respect of persons with God."* In the Scriptures above, there are no situational circumstances—sin is sin, and wrong is wrong. However, let's add balance to that. Just because someone is caught in a fault doesn't give us the right to impose punishment based on our perception immediately. In all things, we must consult God. Sometimes, actions merely reflect an internal issue; therefore, addressing the root of the problem might prove more beneficial overall.

The other method is the "impress method," which leverages the adult's compatibility with the young person. For instance, if your child is passionate about music and aspires to be a professional R&B artist, and you were a talented singer in your youth, you now have common ground. As you demonstrate your talent and skill in that area, your child will be impressed, and you'll have their attention.

Use this method to open lines of communication, help your child achieve their goals, and teach them life lessons using that talent or skill.

Parents, your shared DNA gives you an advantage. Use sports, music, and hobbies to impress your children. Today's generation is the "Do It" generation. Their motto is "Don't talk about it; be about it." They're not interested in past achievements or possessions; they focus solely on the here and now. Your stories won't resonate unless you have something current to show them. To earn the respect of this generation, you must be doing something meaningful right now; otherwise, you're old news.

Drug dealers employ the "impress method" to win over your children, using cars, women, money, clothes, and so forth. And it works. We can't fault the drug dealers entirely; our society prioritizes wealth over the well-being of our children. Many parents work two or three jobs to compete with the wealthy, leaving their children to be raised by unsavory characters. Though our government is structured to perpetuate income inequality, that's irrelevant in leadership. If you're committed to helping your child maximize their potential, you'll do whatever it takes, even if that means sacrificing an eighty-thousand-dollar job requiring sixty to sixty-five hours a week.

Respect, like any other virtue, requires maintenance. The effort it takes to earn respect will undoubtedly equal—or even greater than—the effort needed to maintain it. Consider Michael Jordan, who earned the respect of his NBA peers as the best basketball player of all time. Even before retirement, he had to work tirelessly to keep that respect. Although he's no longer playing, the respect he garnered wasn't solely based on his on-court performance; it also derived from his character and off-court activities.

The process of earning and maintaining respect is crucial for any relationship. These methods have proven effective for me in interactions with both men and women, young and old while serving with youth and adults in the Army. Remember, each person is unique; understanding them is key to achieving optimal results. Whether it's your child, an employee, or any other individual you interact with, they could be the next great inventor, president, astronomer, musician, basketball star, or doctor. Earning their respect requires patience, consistency, and persistence.

So, where did I derive this ideology? Naturally, I borrowed it from the greatest leader: Jesus, our example. According to the Bible, Luke 5:1–11 states:

"Now it came to pass, that, as the people pressed upon him to hear the word of God, he stood by the lake of Gennesaret, And saw two ships standing by the lake: but the fishermen were gone out of them, and were washing their nets. And he entered into one of the ships, which was Simon's, and prayed him that he would thrust out a little from the land. And he sat down, and taught the people out of the ship. Now when he had left speaking, he said unto Simon, Launch out into the deep, and let down your nets for a draught. And Simon answering said unto him, Master, we have toiled all the night, and have taken nothing: nevertheless at thy word I will let down the net. And when they had this done, they inclosed a great multitude of fishes: and their net brake. And they beckoned unto their partners, which were in the other ship, that they should come and help them. And they came, and filled both the ships, so that they began to sink. When Simon Peter saw it, he fell down at Jesus' knees, saying, Depart from me; for I am a sinful man, O Lord. For he was astonished, and all that were with him, at the draught of the fishes which they had taken: And so was also James, and John, the sons of Zebedee, which were partners with Simon. And Jesus said unto Simon, Fear not; from henceforth thou shalt catch men. And when they had brought their ships to land, they forsook all, and followed him." (King James Version)

Jesus used what was important to Peter, James, and John—their fishing skills—to earn their respect. This serves as a lesson for us in identifying what matters to others and, through God's power, earning their respect by setting an example in those areas. You can't afford to live in a bubble, assuming the world revolves around you. Genuine concern for what is essential to others may be the key to earning their respect. What someone can do for themselves, they may do for you. Just as Peter, James, and John were willing to use their fishing skills in the Kingdom of God, a young artist in your youth group might create designs for your events. Your daughter may even assist you in your home business. Regardless of the specifics, you must first earn their respect to bring out their best.

2

ESTABLISHING RELATIONSHIP

This step establishes a foundation for gradually moving into greater responsibility. Both you and your disciple, child, or employee must understand the fine line between business and pleasure. They must realize that while they are taking on more responsibility, you, as the leader, remain in charge. Accomplish this step through the delegation of responsibilities and rewards. Exercise discretion in determining what your disciple, child, or employee can handle. This principle welcomes them into a closer, more mature relationship with you.

I do not mean to suggest you become friends where disrespect is tolerated. Remember, you remain the leader. Even within a friendship, someone must assume the role of responsibility. However, lines of communication are open; use this to your advantage. Adults often say, "I've been there, done that." Some young people find this response unsatisfying. They need to hear about your actual experiences—your failures and successes. We adults have often been guilty of ignoring generational curses—or, as some call them, generational patterns. Some patterns persist from generation to generation because no one has been bold enough to challenge tradition.

A prime example of a generational curse is alcoholism. Perhaps your father was an alcoholic, and you grew up watching him drink his life away. Instead of breaking the pattern, you became an alcoholic, too. Yet you can break this cycle. If not for yourself, then do it for future generations. If you had your child as a teenager, ensure that your child doesn't make the same mistake. Engage them in conversation; explain how it affected your life and the dreams you had to postpone.

Many of my family's generational curses were broken. My parents shattered the cycles of alcoholism and divorce. However, one pattern persisted: having children out of wedlock. My parents warned me, but I didn't listen and ended up having my first son before marriage. This realization hit me much later in life when my drive to achieve my dreams seemed at odds with my family's responsibilities. I spoke to my parents about balancing life and aspirations; their advice was transformative. My family life improved dramatically once I put their guidance into practice. You likely have your own examples—drugs, divorce, adultery, or physical abuse. Don't let the next generation fall victim to these generational curses.

Earlier in this chapter, I mentioned delegating adult responsibilities and rewards. Remember, parents know their children best. Only you can determine what qualifies as an "adult" for your child. However, this is an invaluable part of your relationship with your young person. Your teenager will feel both respected and trusted. So, what do I mean by adult responsibilities and rewards? I'm not talking about mowing the lawn or cleaning a room. I'm referring to tasks like taking charge of the kitchen. Your child manages the cleanliness and operation of the kitchen. This entails creating a roster that includes the duties of every household member, yourself included. They ensure everyone fulfills their assigned tasks and are responsible for operating all appliances. While I wouldn't recommend letting them play the role of repairperson, they should consult you on appliance budgets and arrange for necessary repairs. Most teenagers who resist authority seek some level of it; don't shut them down.

Teach your teenagers how to be leaders. They can learn to both follow and lead. Most will appreciate some degree of authority as a learning opportunity. By implementing this step, you prepare your teenager for adulthood. Fathers, teach your sons the responsibilities of fatherhood. Mothers, do the same for your daughters. They will feel respected and extend that respect back to you. Jesus addresses this in John 15:14–16: *"Ye are my friends, if ye do whatsoever I command you. Henceforth I call you not servants; for the servant knoweth not what his lord doeth: but I have called you friends; for all things that I have heard of my Father I have made known unto you"* (King James Version).

In the early stages of a child's life, you can't always explain everything or answer all questions. Sometimes, children need to respond obediently because you are the authority figure. Immediate, unquestioned obedience can be lifesaving in certain situations. For instance, if your four-year-old runs into the street to chase a ball and a car approaches, you'd do what any parent or authority figure should: shout the child's name and instruct them to stop and come back. You won't have time to explain why; your child's life could be saved because of their trained immediate response.

In the text, Jesus says, *"I no longer call you servants, because a servant does not know his master's business. Instead, I have called you friends"* (John 15:15, NIV). Why? Because you are now mature enough to understand what I am doing. He then elaborates on why he now refers to the disciples as friends rather than servants: "I have taught you everything that I have learned from my Father."

Adults must not make the mistake of withholding vital knowledge from their children. I'm not suggesting you disclose every personal flaw; however, sharing some of your experiences can significantly strengthen your relationship with your teenager. You were a teenager once—you know the desperation to test your ideas, limits, and methods. They'll find appreciation elsewhere if their creativity and fresh insights aren't appreciated at home.

I view a child's life in three stages. From zero to six, you teach through verbal instruction; from six to twelve, you teach through demonstration; and from twelve to eighteen, you teach through practical exercise. Many of us treat our teenagers as if they're devoid of knowledge or insight. If you were to sit down and listen to these young people's perspectives, you might be surprised.

Every generation has witnessed rebellion. We, as adults, have not been wise enough to learn from history. I saw this firsthand during my military service. A friend of mine became my supervisor, and I had to navigate the fine line between business and pleasure. During work hours, he was due the respect accorded to a higher-ranking officer; after hours, we returned to being friends.

This is precisely what your teenager needs to understand: the ability to adapt to situational circumstances. For instance, if I, as an adult, inquire about an unfinished task, the teenager should recognize my authority and respond accordingly. In contrast, while watching a game together, they should be capable of recognizing the relaxed setting and behaving appropriately.

3

DIRECTION FOR LIFE

By the time your child becomes a teenager, I hope you have achieved a level of success that equips you to guide them toward their own successful path. I firmly believe that many teenagers and young adults flounder in school or life because they lack engagement in activities that bring them joy. Imagine the misery of being forced to engage in endeavors that hold no interest for you. Consider, for example, the practice in Germany, where everyone is compelled to serve in the military for two years after high school. While I am a staunch advocate of the benefits of military service, I recognize that it's not for everyone. People can adapt, but adaptation doesn't guarantee happiness or the realization of full potential. To maximize your teenager's productivity, you must identify their passion. What motivates them? What do they excel at and enjoy? These questions are crucial to their success.

For instance, a young man once on my work crew, a bona fide country boy, exhibited profound enthusiasm when we were tasked with removing drywall at a woman's farm. Understanding the project's details, he eagerly shared his previous experience in similar tasks with family members. Recognizing his expertise, I put him in charge of instructing others and ensuring the work's quality. He excelled, completing the job ahead of schedule and displaying an uncharacteristic zeal.

Our educational systems are failing many children. Not everyone aspires to be a doctor, lawyer, or college professor. Some find fulfillment in trades, such as mechanics, plumbing, electrical work, art, computer technology, sales, or landscaping. The key to job satisfaction often lies not in the paycheck but in passion for the position.

Consider a young woman I had the privilege of working with. Talented and eye-catching, she unfortunately had a disruptive attitude. Identifying a role that suited her organizational skills helped channel her energy more positively. I suggested she consider a career in administration, where her outgoing personality could serve her well. After this redirection, our professional relationship improved, and she became an invaluable team member.

The key to your teenager's success lies in identifying their unique passions, gifts, and talents. Owing to genetic similarities, you are ideally positioned to mentor your teenager. Gifted singers often beget gifted singers, just as skilled doctors often produce skilled doctors.

This journey of discovery should be a rewarding experience for both you and your teenager as you explore the passions, gifts, and talents your teen may possess. Identify which of these they want to pursue and guide them in preparing for a potential career opportunity.

Consider this spiritual and natural law: Apples have seeds, which produce more apples of the same kind. The Bible tells us, *"And God said, Let the earth bring forth the living creature after his kind, cattle, and creeping thing, and beast of the earth after his kind: and it was so. And God made the beast of the earth after his kind, and cattle after their kind, and every thing that creepeth upon the earth after his kind: and God saw that it was good,"* (Genesis 1:24–25, KJV).

The key to understanding this verse lies in recognizing that every creature, including humans, is designed to reproduce after its kind. Our children often resemble us and possess many of the same gifts, talents, and abilities. With this understanding, you, as the parent, form the foundation of identity for your teenager. Explore your lineage, examine the traits and skills within your family, and use this information to help your teenager find their place in the world.

Most of my adult family members work in social services. Both of my parents were employed by the school system, as were my uncle and three aunts. My grandmother was a counselor. Virtually all my family is involved in ministry. On my mother's side, most are involved in law enforcement, the military, or corrections. Now, I understand why I joined the Army and loved it. After leaving the Army, all I wanted to do was help people. Parents, your teenager is likely to enjoy what you enjoy and excel in the areas where you excel. Explore yourself and aid your young person in finding their place in this world.

4

BE THEIR BIGGEST FAN

One thing a teenager will not refuse is a cheering section. In a teenager's life, performance plays a significant role—the number of friends you have and the support you receive often hinge on your performance. Given performance's pivotal role in a teenager's life, parents and leaders have an excellent avenue for involvement. What motivates our young people to perform at such high levels? Primarily, it's the desire for approval, praise, and acceptance from friends and family.

Approval, praise, and acceptance are the key drivers behind teenagers' eagerness and aggressiveness concerning their performance. If parents were to praise their children as much as—or even more than—their children's friends, the struggle for our children's well-being would almost cease. In my experience with teenagers, it has become increasingly apparent that self-esteem is a significant issue, especially among females. This problem stems from inadequate grade point averages (GPAs) and insufficient quality time fathers spend with their daughters.

In dealing with female teenagers, I have realized the importance of emotional security. The strongest part of a female is her emotions;

she endures the pain of childbirth out of love for her unborn child. When interacting with females, you must cater to their emotional needs. They should feel safe and secure with you. How can this be achieved? One thing teenagers—and children—can detect is whether you genuinely care about them. You must help them understand you are there for them, not for personal gain. This is the key to winning a female's trust.

When meeting a female for the first time, I usually inquire about her interests and aspirations. Her responses might surprise you, but she will be intrigued by your interest. As I learn more about her, I praise my observation's positive aspects. Sometimes, I even commend the negatives. I once knew a young woman who was an exceptional debater. Despite her talent, she argued with a young man about why women shouldn't perform certain tasks. For every point the young man expressed, she had a counterpoint. I told her she should study to become a lawyer, praising her ability to introduce doubt into the young man's arguments. Like algebra, we should focus on transforming negatives into positives.

Consider many of today's highly regarded superstars. I wonder who praised and approved of their performances during their younger days. Michael Jordan's story is particularly relevant. Often regarded as the greatest basketball player of all time, Jordan was once cut from his high school basketball team. Yet someone believed in him—his father. Jordan's journey, fraught with struggles and trials, would not have been the same without the crucial support of his father and other key figures. His success resulted from two factors: First, Michael discovered his passion and talent and pursued them as a career; second, his family provided the necessary praise, approval, and acceptance. The story of Michael Jordan serves as a perfect example of these two factors working in harmony.

As a teenager, I was rebellious and often found trouble. Being the oldest of three boys, with an elder sister, I was the troublemaker in the group. Despite my rebellious nature, some people said I could have become a lawyer due to my knack for arguing. Unfortunately, during my teenage years, I seldom heard positive praise. My friends amply praised my negative actions, driving me further down that path. Eventually, I joined the Army, where I learned to respect authority. This experience shaped me into an outstanding soldier, and my need for external praise gradually diminished. I established my own high standards.

I am married and have three children; life is going well. However, I overlooked the impact of others' praise and approval until my father expressed approval of my family life. That day was probably one of the happiest days of my life—my wife would attest to it. Even though I hadn't given him many reasons to praise or approve of me as a teenager, it was something I deeply desired. Although I claimed to be independent, I realized that my father's approval was essential to elevating my family's standards.

Working with a young man at a local boot camp, I understood how much a little praise could help. Although his group did not win the competition, I praised them for their effort. While serving in Iraq a year later, I received a letter from this young man who was in trouble again. He mentioned he would never forget me because, despite losing the competition, I was proud of them. This experience helped me realize the power of praise, approval, and acceptance in motivating teenagers.

Luke 10:23–24 says, *"And he turned him unto his disciples, and said privately, Blessed are the eyes which see the things that ye see: For I tell you, that many prophets and kings have desired to see those things which ye see, and have not seen them; and to hear those things which ye hear, and have not heard them"* (King James Version). This is an example of Jesus praising the seventy disciples for their success in ministry. Praise should be personal, highlighting the unique abilities of the person performing. Individuals must know that they are unique and one of a kind; there are no copies in humankind.

5

NEVER GIVE UP

By the time your teenager reaches twelve, you can bet they have difficulty trusting people. Contrary to popular belief, adults must earn the trust of teenagers experiencing problems. If your teenager has been in trouble for most of their life, they've seen people who claimed to care about them come and go. The worst thing you can do is quit on your teenager. Although your child is no longer connected to you through the umbilical cord, they remain emotionally and spiritually connected.

Take, for instance, a young woman I knew who was having problems with her children. She was a devout Christian. On days she forgot to read her Bible, her children seemed to behave at their worst. Her daily Bible reading set the pace for a smoother day. But when her day didn't go as planned, it appeared her children lost their minds. They were small then, but the emotional and spiritual connection between a parent and a child transcends age. Often, your emotional state is transmitted to your children. If you're depressed, they may pick up on that depression. They don't have to react to depression in the same way, but that doesn't mean they haven't internalized it.

Parenting is one of the most challenging tasks anyone can undertake. To parent effectively, you must balance your child physically, emotionally, and spiritually. It's crucial to do your best to develop a well-rounded child. You wouldn't want your child to mature physically and spiritually while emotionally they are still in their infancy. Third John 1:2 says, *"Beloved, I pray that all may go well with you and that you may be in good health, just as it is well with your soul"* (King James Version). This scripture implies that we should mature or prosper in all aspects of life at the same rate.

Consider the challenges in raising a child with developmental disabilities. The patience and love required extend to making this child the center of their parent's universe. Yet, they never quit. Many of these parents continue to care for their mentally challenged children into adulthood. This commitment can keep a teenager's will to survive and stay alive.

I recall a young man with whom I worked. He was relatively large and occasionally disrupted my crew, mainly for attention. I used push-ups as a discipline. When I first met this young man, he couldn't do any push-ups. But I told him I believed he could. He would roll around on the ground, cry, and try to catch my attention to let him off the hook. I told him he wouldn't get up until he completed at least half the required push-ups. He completed the push-ups not out of fear of being on the ground all day (he had experienced that before) but because he knew I was committed to his completing those push-ups. My belief in him and my refusal to quit on him helped him master the task. About a year after this experience, he wrote me a letter, recalling this incident and thanking me for believing in him.

Words of praise and compliments are necessary, but teenagers will watch your actions. They will test your commitment. You must pass that test. If you continue to parent with the mindset, "I'm an adult, and my child should just do what I tell them," you'll likely face ongoing rebellion from your teen. The act of giving and receiving is crucial. Show your teens you are committed to parenting them and will pay any price. Once you've proven your commitment, your child will, in return, commit to you.

How do you show your commitment? One way is to express your frustration positively. Don't be afraid to express disappointment but assure them you're always there for them when all is said and done. Speak to them about your frustrations, but ensure they understand you are not giving up. Never give up; your child's survival may depend on your commitment.

CONCLUSION

The intent of this book is not to offer leaders a foolproof, step-by-step formula for guiding their followers. Each individual exhibits a unique blend of personality, character, spirit, physicality, and emotion. What motivates one person may not motivate another; what works for one may not work for another. However, I am of the conviction that, at their core, all people desire the same things. While their methods of acquisition may differ, their wants remain consistent. What do they desire? Love, respect, praise, approval, and leadership are just a few universal human desires. Parenting is akin to leadership, and leadership is akin to parenting. It is incumbent upon you to prepare individuals for their life tasks. God has preordained every individual to contribute something of value to this world and His kingdom. As leaders, our responsibility is to assist people in discovering their destined paths and help them fulfill their purpose. This pursuit of purpose is where true happiness originates.

Consider the purpose of a chair: it is designed for sitting. Its longevity is jeopardized if used for a purpose other than sitting. The same principle applies to every human being on Earth. God has meticulously designed us to fulfill a specific destiny. If we fail to walk that destined path, our chances of living a fulfilled and joyful life dwindle.

These five steps will prove invaluable as you mold the future generation, a critical component of our nation's future. Among your followers, there may be the next pioneering inventor, the next great President of the United States, or the next groundbreaking astronomer, scientist, evangelist, doctor, lawyer, scholar, basketball star, musician, psychologist, sociologist, youth leader, author, soldier, firefighter, police officer, carpenter, computer technician, etc. Utilize these five steps to transform the rebellious, argumentative, and irresponsible individual into a highly motivated and productive team member, ready and equipped to fulfill their purpose with confidence, discipline, and direction. God bless.

According to the U.S. Census Bureau, twenty-four million children in America—one out of three—live in biological father-absent homes. Consequently, a "father factor" exists in nearly all the social issues facing America today. Children in father-absent homes are almost four times more likely to be poor. In 2011, twelve percent of children in married-couple families lived in poverty, compared with forty-four percent in mother-only families.

Source: U.S. Census Bureau, Children's Living Arrangements and Characteristics: March 2011, Table C8. Washington, D.C.: 2011.

In 2008, American poverty rates were 13.2 percent for the whole population and nineteen percent for children, compared to 28.7 percent for female-headed households.

Source: Edin, K., & Kissane, R. J. (2010). Poverty and the American Family: A Decade in Review. Journal of Marriage and Family, 72, 460–479.

Data from three waves of the Fragile Families Study (N = 2,111) were used to examine the prevalence and effects of mothers' relationship changes between birth and age three on their children's well-being. Children born to single mothers show higher levels of aggressive behavior than children born to married mothers. Living in a single-mother household is equivalent to experiencing 5.25 partnership transitions.

Source: Osborne, C., & McLanahan, S. (2007). Partnership Instability and Child Well-being. Journal of Marriage and Family, 69, 1065–1083.

A sample of 4,027 resident fathers and children from the Fragile Families and Child Well-Being Survey was used to investigate the effects of a biological father's multi-partner fertility on adolescent health. Resident fathers engaging in multi-partner fertility were older and more likely to be white. They had lower education levels and income than fathers with one partner. In addition, results indicated children's externalizing behaviors were negatively affected directly and indirectly when their biological father had children with multiple partners.

Source: Bronte-Tinkew, J., Horowitz, A., & Scott, M. E. (2009). Fathering with Multiple Partners: Links to Children's Well-being in Early Childhood. Journal of Marriage and Family, 71, 608–631.

Infant mortality rates are 1.8 times higher for infants of unmarried mothers than for infants of married mothers.

Source: Matthews, T. J., Sally C. Curtin, and Marian F. MacDorman. Infant Mortality Statistics from the 1998 Period Linked Birth/Infant Death Data Set. National Vital Statistics Reports, Vol. 48, No. 12. Hyattsville, MD: National Center for Health Statistics, 2000.

High-quality interaction by any type of father predicts better infant health.

Source: Carr, D., & Springer, K. W. (2010). Advances in Families and Health Research in the 21st Century. Journal of Marriage and Family, 72, 743–761.

Even after controlling for income, youths in father-absent households still had significantly higher odds of incarceration than those in mother-father families. In addition, youths who never had a father in the household experienced the highest odds.

Source: Harper, Cynthia C., and Sara S. McLanahan. "Father Absence and Youth Incarceration." Journal of Research on Adolescence 14 (September 2004): 369–397.

A 2002 Department of Justice survey of seven thousand inmates revealed that thirty-nine percent of jail inmates lived in mother-only households. Approximately forty-six percent of jail inmates in 2002 had a previously incarcerated family member. One-fifth experienced a father in prison or jail.

Source: James, Doris J. Profile of Jail Inmates, 2002. (NCJ 201932). Bureau of Justice Statistics Special Report, Department of Justice, Office of Justice Programs, July 2004.

A study of 109 juvenile offenders indicated that family structure significantly predicts delinquency.

Source: Bush, Connee, Ronald L. Mullis, and Ann K. Mullis. "Differences in Empathy Between Offender and Nonoffender Youth." Journal of Youth and Adolescence 29 (August 2000): 467–478.

A study of low-income minority adolescents aged ten to fourteen found that higher social encounters and frequent communication with nonresident biological fathers decreased adolescent delinquency.

Source: Coley, R. L., & Medeiros, B. L. (2007). *Reciprocal Longitudinal Relations Between Nonresident Father Involvement and Adolescent Delinquency*. Child Development, 78, 132–147.

Being raised by a single mother increases the risk of teen pregnancy, marrying with less than a high school degree, and forming a marriage in which both partners have less than a high school degree.

Source: Teachman, Jay D. "The Childhood Living Arrangements of Children and the Characteristics of Their Marriages." *Journal of Family Issues* 25 (January 2004): 86-111.

Fifty-seven point six percent of Black children, thirty-one point two percent of Hispanic children, and twenty-point seven percent of white children live apart from their biological fathers.

Source: *Family Structure and Children's Living Arrangements 2012.* Current Population Report. U.S. Census Bureau, July 1, 2012.

A study using data from the Fragile Families and Child Well-Being Study revealed that, in many cases, the absence of a biological father contributes to an increased risk of child maltreatment. The results suggest that Child Protective Services (CPS) agencies have some justification for viewing a social father as increasing children's risk of abuse and neglect. It is believed that in families with a non-biological (social) father figure, there is a higher risk of abuse and neglect of children, despite the social father living in the household or only dating the mother.

Source: "CPS Involvement in Families with Social Fathers." *Fragile Families Research Brief No. 46.* Princeton, NJ, and New York, NY: Bendheim-Thomas Center for Research on Child Well-being and Social Indicators Survey Center, 2010.

In a study examining factors related to maternal physical-child-abuse risk, researchers interviewed mothers of three-year-old children. The results revealed that mothers married to fathers were at a lower risk of maternal physical child abuse. Moreover, higher educational attainment and positive father involvement were significant predictors of a lower maternal physical-child-abuse risk.

Source: Guterman, N.B., Yookyong, L., Lee, S.J., Waldfogel, J., & Rathouz, P.J. (2009). *Fathers and Maternal Risk for Physical Child Abuse.* Child Maltreatment, 14, 277–290.

In a study of six thousand five hundred children from the ADDHEALTH database, father closeness was negatively correlated with the number of a child's friends who smoke, drink, and use marijuana. Closeness was also correlated with a child's use of alcohol, cigarettes, and hard drugs and was linked to family structure. Intact families ranked higher in father closeness than did single-parent families.

Source: National Fatherhood Initiative. "Family Structure, Father Closeness, & Drug Abuse." Gaithersburg, MD: National Fatherhood Initiative, 2004: 20–22.

In an assessment of four thousand one hundred nine two-parent families, researchers examined the effects of early maternal and paternal depression on child expressive language at age twenty-four months. The study also explored the role that parent-to-child reading might play in a child's language development. Results indicated that, for both mothers and fathers, depressive symptoms were negatively associated with parent-to-child reading. Only for fathers, however, was earlier depression associated with later reading to the child and subsequent child expressive vocabulary development. The fewer the times fathers read to their infants, the lower the toddlers scored on a standard measure of expressive vocabulary at age two. Furthermore, parents' depression affected how often fathers read to their children more than it did mothers, thereby influencing the child's language development.

Source: Paulson, J.F., Keefe, H.A., & Leiferman, J.A. (2009). *Early Parental Depression and Child Language Development*. Journal of Child Psychology and Psychiatry, 50, 254–262.

ABOUT THE AUTHOR

Apostle Terry Stephens II is a powerful apostolic and prophetic leader used by God to usher in a fresh perspective concerning Kingdom government and leadership. His mission is to unite the body of Christ for the last days' stand. He operates with a unique, revelatory anointing that focuses on breaking the chains of religion and tradition. With a military perspective, Apostle Stephens is passionate about fivefold-ministry leadership aligned with a Kingdom agenda.

While serving in the United States Army and deployed to Iraq, God began imparting the vision for Truth & Wholeness Ministries to Apostle Stephens. Guided by the Spirit of God, Truth & Wholeness Ministries aims to resemble the Army through cultural diversity, developing leaders, and establishing a distinct Kingdom culture. The ministry was founded in June 2011 and continues to grow and expand its reach.

Apostle Stephens has a heart for the prodigal sons and daughters of the Kingdom and is committed to delivering a message of restoration to all who will listen. He is a Network of Local Churches (NLC) member, established by Apostle Lafayette Scales of Rhema Christian Center in Columbus, Ohio. He founded T&W Publishing and authored *Jesus Our Fivefold Ministry Leader*, released in March 2012. His works include *Kingdom Equipment 101: Tools for Kingdom Purpose, God's Business Plan, Biblical Prescriptions For Life's Troubles, and Discipline and Direction: God's Leadership Style.*

Passionate about Kingdom leadership and team ministry, Apostle Stephens founded the Dad Leadership Group in 2015. This small business specializes in coaching, consulting, and leadership development, enhancing community-based organizations, churches, and leaders at all levels. In 2016, God led him to change the name of Truth & Wholeness Ministries to Manifestation Church, which focused on training individuals to manifest sonship.

In 2020, he and his wife, Janet Stephens, launched the nonprofit organization Bridges to Life Community Services. Their mission is to serve the urban community, build families, and connect resources. As a twenty-five-year military veteran, Apostle Stephens views his calling as a spiritual boot camp, where he nurtures Kingdom citizens, equips them for wholeness, and then sends them forth for Kingdom advancement. Alongside his wife, Lady Janet Stephens, and their blended family of six children—Janeyce, Janique, Tre, Jaylin, Andre, and Maya—Apostle Stephens is on a mission to ensure that all individuals realize the abundant life that Jesus came to offer.

ALSO BY TERRY STEPHENS

Kingdom Equipment 101: Tools for Kingdom Purpose

God's Business Plan

Biblical Prescriptions For Life's Troubles

www.ingramcontent.com/pod-product-compliance
Lightning Source LLC
Chambersburg PA
CBHW070955120626
46546CB00004B/1621